# *Shadows of My Father*

## *A Poetic Journey*

**Colleen Keller Breuning**

***"Shadows of My Father"***
***Colleen Keller Breuning © 2011***



Blue Turtle Press
Plantation, Florida
Purcellville, Virginia

Websites:
http://colleenbreuning.com
http://www.blueturtlecrossing.com
http://www.facebook.com/colleen.breuning
http://www.myspace.com/colleenbpoetry
https://twitter.com/#!/colleenbreuning
https://plus.google.com/u/0/111518879309560628213/posts

Blogs:
http://colleenbreuning.wordpress.com/
http://thesunsetpoet.blogspot.com/
http://colleenbreuning./tumblelog/tumbler.com/

Contact: cmbreuning@gmail.com



ISBN: 978-0-9836072-0-6
ISBN-13: 978-0-9836072-0-5

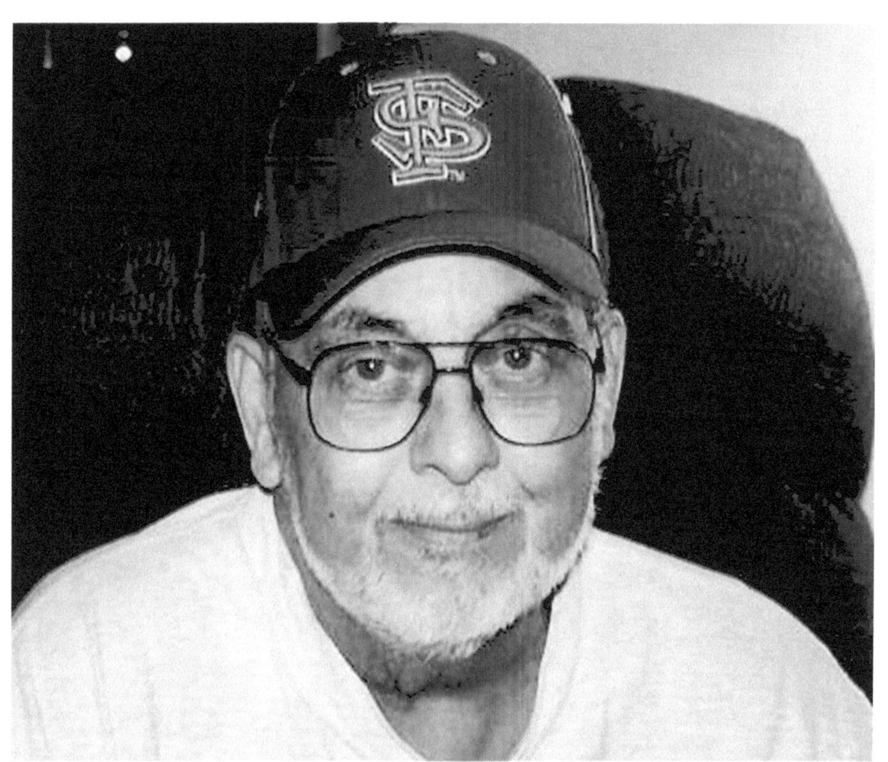

## ***Dedication***

*This book is dedicated to the memory of my dearly beloved father, Philip Thomas Keller, who died on February 17, 2003, from metastatic lung cancer.*

*My father was one of fourteen children who grew up during the Depression in western Maryland. He was a strong and silent man who worked for the railroad, just like his father. His love of music and nature, particularly birds, was a constant source of inspiration to me.*

*I returned to writing poetry in an attempt to deal with the overwhelming grief that I experienced after my father's death.*

*Dad, I love you, I miss you, and I think of you every single day. However, I take comfort in knowing you are my very own guardian angel watching over me from heaven! Until we meet again…*

*With all my love,*
*Colleen*

# Table of Contents

# Table of Contents

## Acknowledgments

*First and foremost, I would like to thank my parents for giving me the precious gift of life. Dad, you are in my heart always. Mom, thank you for your guidance and love over the years. Your strength and unwavering faith are truly amazing. Also, many thanks for proofreading and editing this manuscript. Your eagle eye and your honest input are greatly appreciated. I love you!*

*I am most grateful to my husband Dan for his support and encouragement during my return to writing. Thanks for the gentle push I needed to finally bring this book to fruition. The unconditional love we share has blessed us with good times and enabled us to weather the storms in our lives. I love you with all my heart!*

*Thank you to my children, Vince and Katie, for being the lights in my life. Being your mother is a privilege, and you both fill my heart with joy and gratitude on a daily basis. I love you more than you will ever know!*

*Thanks to Joanne Olivieri, fellow poet, mentor, and friend. Your advice and technical assistance has been invaluable during the publication process.*

*Last but not least, to all my online poet friends out there who have inspired, supported, and encouraged me all these years….*
*Thank you, my kindred spirits! I appreciate your friendship, and I hope to meet you in person some day.*

*Thank you all from the bottom of my heart…..*

*Love,*
*Colleen*

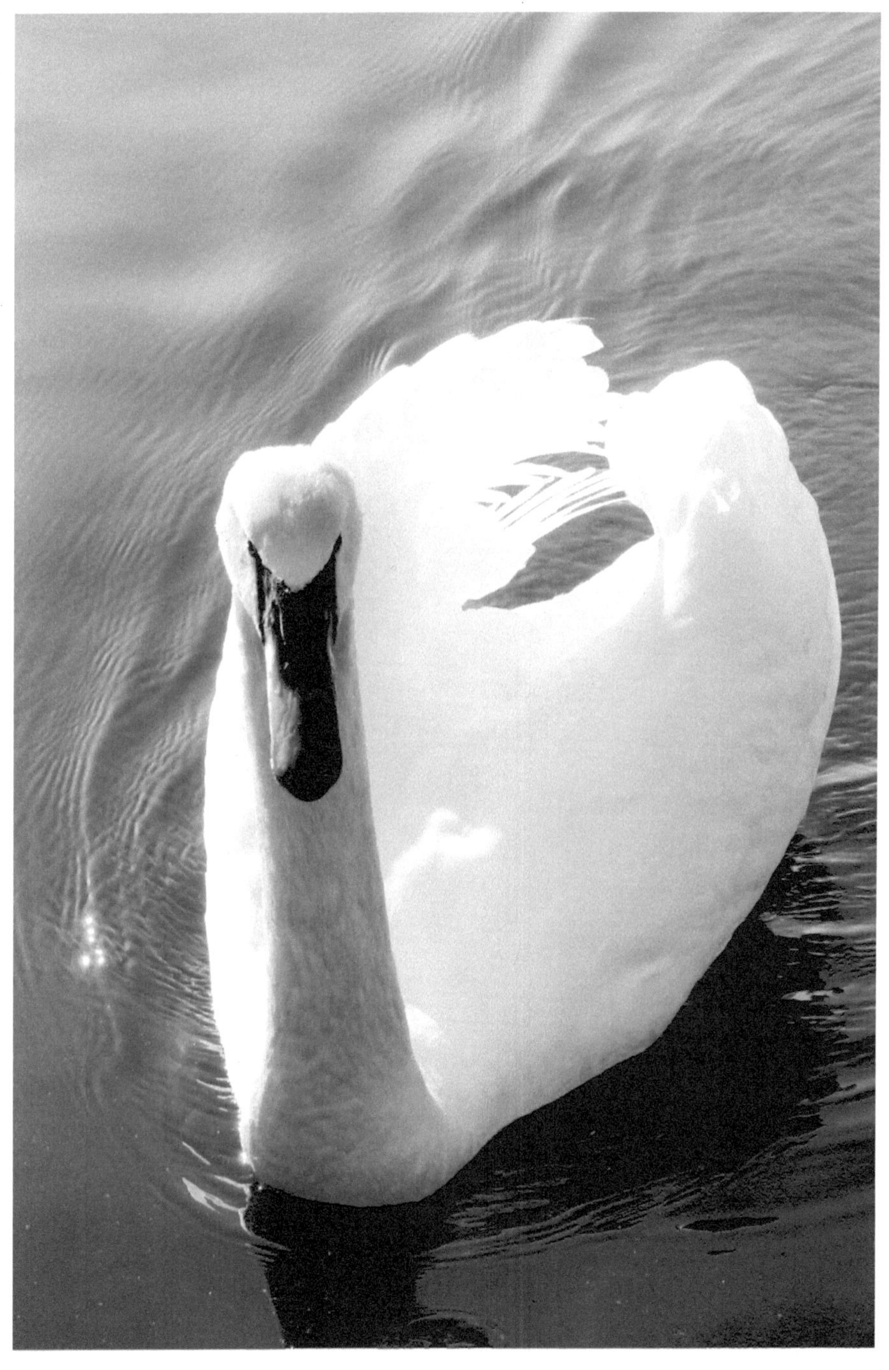

***"Courage is grace under pressure."***

Ernest Hemingway

## **Shadows of My Father**

As a child, I walked through the park
hand in hand with my father.
Brimming with energy and innocence,
I played a game of hide and seek,
jumping into his enormous shadow.
My elfin figure was gobbled up
by his lumbering adumbration,
stretching long across the path
illuminated by the springtime sun.

Young and stupid in love,
I felt as if my father's shadow
was falling over me, somehow
supplanted in my subconscious.
Though I could not see it,
I could feel his image lingering,
cutting through the darkness,
watching me as I made mistakes
from which he could not protect me.

I could sense his shadow slipping
away that New Year's Day,
battle weary from the fight of his life.
With a weak smile on his face,
my father gazed at me
from his hospital bed.
I knew from the far away look
in his soft hazel eyes
that I was saying goodbye.

Now as I walk alone
with the sun on my back,
my own blackened silhouette
extends before me.
There are no huge hands to hold,
no large shadows to jump into.
But my soul is at peace,
and I smile, knowing that I carry
his shadow inside of mine.

## I Dream in Color

The winds of summer spark poignant memories:
A cluster of red balloons floating in blue skies,
Catching butterflies with tattered fishing nets,
Delicate velvet wings fluttering before my eyes.

*Hues of crimson, sapphire and jade…*
*I pray the colors of my life never fade.*

My senses come to life and take me back:
The sweet taste of honeysuckle on my tongue,
The scent of freesia lingering in the breeze,
My heart skipping a beat when I was young.

*I could have sworn this was just a dream,*
*But things are not always what they seem.*

Mementos gathered in a steamer trunk:
Stacks of love letters amidst the dust,
Fingering crackled sepia snapshots,
A fabric photo album emanating must.

*Hues of crimson, sapphire and jade…*
*I pray the colors of my life never fade.*

The sky is breaking, rain is pouring down;
My tears of mourning so deftly disguised.
Is that you standing right in front of me?
I try to speak, but my mouth is paralyzed.

*I could have sworn this was just a dream…*
*But things are not always what they seem.*

## Cold Marble

My cheek rests
on cold marble.
Tears leach out
onto the stony pattern
of smoky quartz
and slate gray.

Shoulders heave
and lungs strain
for breath
against the onslaught
of unrelenting sorrow,
which will not cease.

A primitive wail
escapes my throat
and I am drowning,
lost in mourning,
because I can't
have you in my life
anymore.

I cannot lift my head
nor my heart.
Like cold marble,
weighted down,
I am falling,
falling,
falling…
into an endless chasm.

Some days I sit like this
for hours,
my head
upon the cold marble counter,
my heart scored,
my soul drained,
until I feel your presence.

A gentle prod,
your hand on my shoulder,
brings me comfort.
My heart fills up,
destined to survive
another day
without you.

## The Gardener

Every March saw him grow restless --
he felt the rush of spring fever
coursing through his ambitious veins,
evidenced by dog eared Burpee catalogs
and tattered gardener's books
stacked beside the painted pantry.

Strong arthritic fingers dug
into coarse, pungent loam,
pushing tiny seeds deep down,
into a blanket of black compost,
sprinkled with water and love.

In his modest backyard garden
lilac bushes perfumed the air,
purple morning glory caressed
the varnished wooden arbor,
tangerine daylilies waved from beds
beside rows of violet snapdragons,
standing tall, on guard like soldiers.

Robust bell peppers pushed forth
in brilliant hues of green and scarlet,
savory sun-ripened tomato vines
crawled high up wooden stakes
like rogue bladerunners
reaching for the cloudless sky.

But in a cruel twist of fate,
the heartless hands of winter
took the tired gardener
during the bleakest blizzard.

Spring dawned with April rain,
but the tiny garden fell
into inevitable disrepair --
cracked pots of terra cotta
speckled with mud lay
beneath the weathered arbor,

weeds sprouted up, choking
the life out of the seedlings,
leaving once fertile beds
dry and barren.

The latch of the shed has rusted,
but the aluminum door gives way
to tools of his precious trade.
I feel a surge in my restless veins
as I grab the blue-tined rake
and work the dirt, sweating,
sifting out stones, dead roots,
and clumps of dried weeds.

My nimble thin fingers
enrich the beds with loam,
dig trenches to scatter seeds,
rubber boots tamping down soil,
embellishing with cool water
as my heart fills with hope
that life and love will bloom again…

*I can almost smell the lilacs.*

## From the Maryland Skies

You took your last breath on President's Day
As the snow fell gently from the Maryland skies.
One thousand miles away, I was down on my knees...
Teardrops on your photographs, rain from my eyes.

I look to the heavens to search for an answer,
There persists the strands of your mystical presence.
Your smile pulls me from memories, as if from your grave,
Floating peacefully along the ethereal essence.

A childhood of happiness, I simply cannot let go,
Recalling fond moments, rainbows glisten in my tears.
Your eyes were the map that showed me the way,
Beautiful memories of you I shall forever hold dear.

I can still hear you singing sweetly as you strum your ukulele,
Delightful, mystical visions of you, into my dreams they seep.
I can see you looking down at me from your perch in heaven,
Proudly smiling at the wonderful surprises your life did reap.

Sometimes I think I hear you whispering at my window
As the summer night rustles my curtains with its sighs.
I'm falling apart once again, bitter tears soak my pillowcase
As the rain falls gently from the Maryland skies.

## Sadness Passes Through

Wandering through the city park
is like turning the pages
of my childhood scrapbook,
its tattered, familiar pages spread out before me.

Freight trains chugging and whistling in the distance,
Riding banana seat bicycles around the lake,
Eight white swans loping behind us,
Gobbling up trails of stale Wonder Bread crumbs,
Sailing high in the sky on wooden swings,
Legs flailing, hair flying,
Screaming in the summer air,
Sprinting down cobblestone paths,
Tripping over maple tree roots,
Bruised legs, skinned knees,
My blood and tears on your handkerchief.

Now, sitting on the splintered park bench,
I hear the distant trains cry out
and a sadness passes through my heart...

*because I just can't say goodbye.*

## **Primavera**

Weathered hands spread
over faded ivory keys.
The pendulum of the bow
strikes the cello's strings,
cajoling,
coaxing,
caressing,
releasing ribbons of notes
into the atmosphere.

The haunting melodies
of my yesterdays
rise up in my chest,
building to a crescendo
and scaling the peaks
of my fervent emotions.

The jagged passages
tear at the loose stitches
of my scarred heart.
My eyes close tight,
burning against
the brimming tears.

But the music reaches deep
within my being
and clutches my soul,
tossing me into the void
like a tattered shell in a riptide,
caught in the undertow.

The symphony swells,
releasing the torrents
of pent up heartache,
unleashing the flow
of my blood,
unhinging the floodgates
of my broken life…

as I bitterly weep.

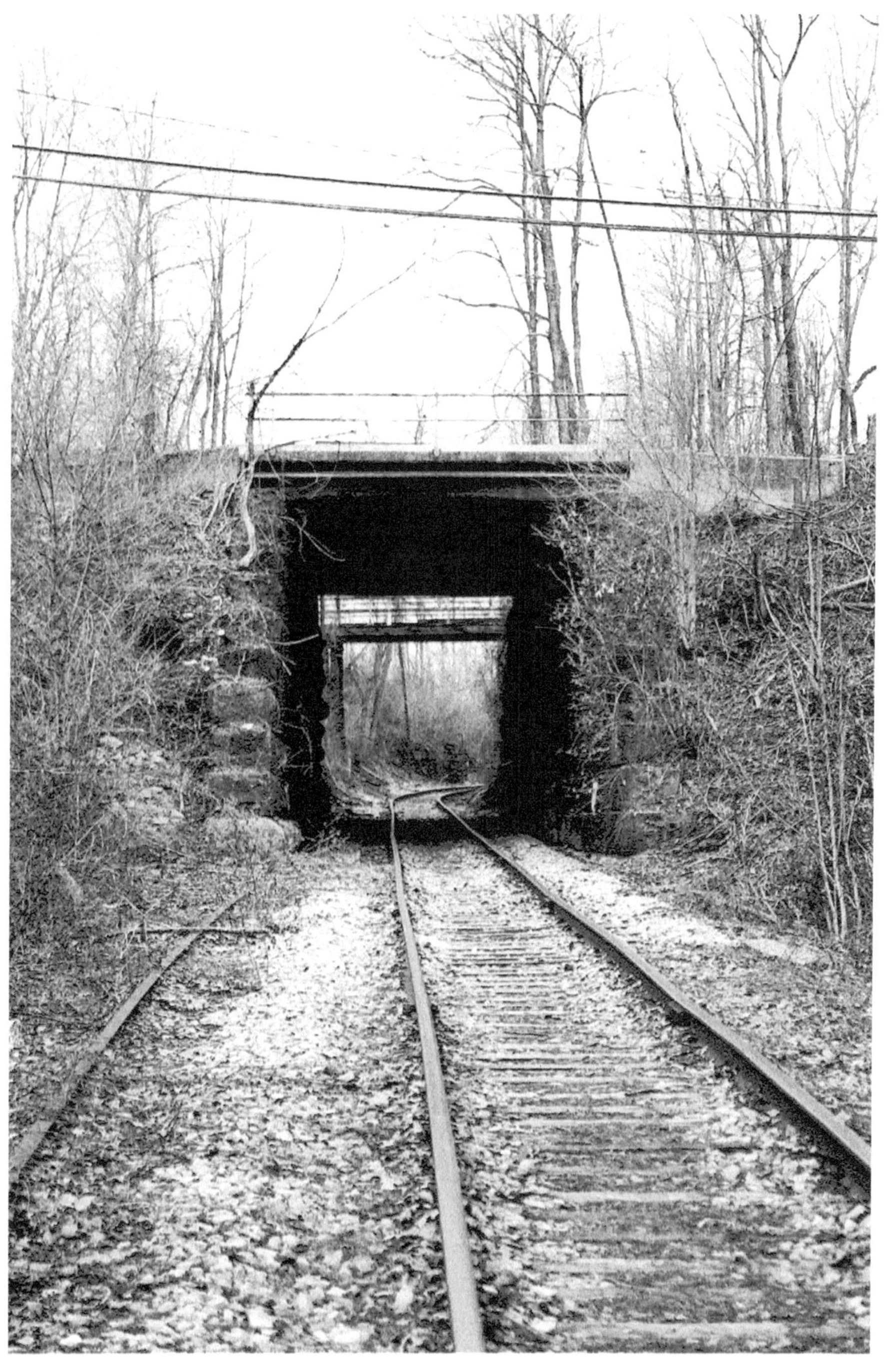

***"Life is a journey that must be traveled no matter how bad the roads and accommodations."***

Oliver Goldsmith

## I Cried A River

One thousand miles away, you lay dying.
Tubes and wires connected your body to beeping monitors,
but I could not reach you. The screams were building up inside,
the pressure squeezed the breath right out of my lungs.
Helpless, hopeless, I could only run in the wind and rain.
I was certain this would be your final day.

Seven orange-breasted robins crossed my path on this trek.
So strange, in all my years I had never seen one robin
fly this far south, the sub-tropics, for the winter.
I remember that we used to watch the robins in the back yard
cavort and pluck fat, pink worms from the ground
so many summers ago. Why did they appear on this day?

Seven times I heard that haunting love song
as I scanned the radio stations for music.
Yet I felt hypnotized and listened each time, as its potent words
sent a spike straight through my heart.
"Go, the damage is done; I guess I'll be leaving."
I cried a river, I lived the song, tears mingling with rain.

Seven miles I raced toward the finish
of what I knew was imminent and inevitable.
My mind tried to reconcile your destiny.
My soul tried to bargain with God.
My heart tried to believe that you heard the words I spoke aloud,
"It's okay, Daddy. You can go. You can go!"

Three years gone, and you are still larger than life to me.
Today you would have been seventy-one.
Today I run, a futile attempt to escape my fears, to ease my pain.
And now my iPod deals me that same damned song. Once again
I cry that river, I live that song.
Tears mingle with sweat as I grieve forever:
I could not hold you and tell you goodbye.

~ *This poem was inspired by my father and the song, "Cry Me A River," by Justin Timberlake. These events actually happened on the day my father died... I wrote this three years after his death, on what would have been his 71st birthday.*

**Shades of Blue**

Time chips away at
The indigo ice
Surrounding my heart,
Melting slowly
Into a puddle
At my feet...

Cool crystal tears
Spill down my face
At the sound of your voice,
I can see the sparkle
Of your aquamarine eyes
In my mind...

And the world seems emptier
Without you...
I'm forever lost in shades of blue,
I'm forever missing you…

Each night the sun descends
From its perch
In cornflower skies
Settling into blankets
Of cumulus clouds,
Giving me hope...

But only time can heal
This gaping hole
In my sapphire soul,
Only time will tell if
You will come back to me,
As the tides ebb and flow...

And I pray I'm one day closer
To seeing you...
I'm forever lost in shades of blue,
I'm forever missing you...

## The Treasure Box

A cigar box of yellowed wood grain sits alone
On his overstuffed burgundy velour chair
Beside the old brick fireplace.
Cardboard lid warped from fingers and time,
Its musty smell gives way to his treasures.

Black and white photographs, crinkled and worn.
Strapping young airman, dress blues and starched hat
Waiting outside on the front porch, chilled,
Lucky Strike cigarette in hand.
Mitch Miller chorus sings of German beer and victory.

Hand made heart-shaped card
Of faded lace and pink construction paper.
Etched in black crayon,
"Be My Valentine, Daddy."
February 1966.

Greetings from Myrtle Beach,
Only five cents at the souvenir shop.
Smooth and glossy, carved in ballpoint blue,
"You kids would love the sandy beach and boardwalk!"
Postcard never sent.

Ebony rosary of smooth onyx beads,
Polished and cool to the touch.
Black carved crucifix, life-like Jesus
Smells of old wood and musk,
Handed down from Uncle Bobby.

Family snapshots from the Instamatic:
Amber cat eyeglasses, gold plaid seventies jacket,
Kelly green polyester pantsuit, saddle shoes.
As Neil Diamond serenaded Cracklin' Rosie,
We laughed until our sides hurt and tears flowed.

Captiva chestnut conch shell, swirls of creamy pink;
Eight points surround the center like a sun.
The briny scent of ocean and sand remains.
Plucked from the tumbling surf as I prayed --
A sign from God.

His treasure box now sits on the drafty hearth
Beside his now empty burgundy chair.
I lay the shell upon your resting place in the snow.
Eyes stinging, I pray for your repose…

*See you in Captiva, Daddy.*

## Gilded Wings

The heavens hang
a laundry line of clouds
as far as the eye can see,
where placid waters
meet the sky.
The gentle tumble of breakers,
languid whispers
like velvet…
a soft caress
upon my ears
reminding me
of long ago.

Summer days that stretched
like bent and broken limbs,
reaching across
gray linen fields
for the temporal sun,
forever beckoning
with its white-hot light.

But my dreams
dissolved….
I was not unlike Icarus
in his doomed attempt
to fly….
I hovered
ever closer
to your heart
of radiant beams.
I too, have melted,
like those gilded wings,
imperfect, wilting.

Perhaps it was my destiny
to melt, to dissolve
in a puddle of wax at your feet,
a fallen angel who veered
from her righteous path
on the way
to eternity.

## Raindrops

From every raindrop falling
and floating out to sea,
I hear the gentle voice of God
calling after me.

The scent of lilacs in the air,
the rustle of the pines,
the rain upon majestic mountains –
His presence is divine.

The broken days seem daunting,
and troubles take their toll.
As cooling raindrops touch my face,
His presence soothes my soul.

The raindrops are relentless;
they spill down all day long.
Lucid, liquid angels from above,
they whisper His sweet song.

The raindrops' journey is complete,
from heavenly clouds to sea.
The gentle grace of God has filled my soul,
His love has set me free.

## **Dream Catcher**

I stretch my arms high overhead
Toward dappled amethyst skies,
Reaching ever closer to the sun,
Far beyond where the eagle flies.

I am hunting down sweet dreams
To catch in my delicate feathered net.
Distant memories of my childhood,
Times that I cannot bear to forget.

I close my eyes and count to ten
As the sunlight fades to black.
To the inner recesses of my brain,
My imagination takes me back.

We are riding on the painted ponies;
I, with golden daisies in my hair.
The carousel spins ever faster,
Calliope music tinkling in the air.

Counting boxcars at the station,
We walk down roughshod railroad tracks.
Our breath like smoke against the cold,
The bitter breeze pushing at our backs.

From the sanctity of my sleep,
A cacophony of sound awakens me…
Like ten thousand foreign voices
Pleading with me desperately.

What is this chatter in the wind,
This logorrhea of nonsense streaming?
A band of angels pushes me onward,
Telling me to keep on dreaming.

I struggle to find my paradise lost,
But nothing is the same since you died.
Yet I know I only have to think of you
And I can feel you here by my side.

So I'll reach high across the heavens,
Skimming through God's works of art
To catch precious dreams of childhood
And store them safe inside my heart.

## The Lankford Hotel

On hot August nights
he sits on the spindle-back rocking chair
on the third floor balcony
of the Lankford Hotel…
rocking, gently rocking,
with the easterly breeze
upon his face.

On hot August nights
the boardwalk lies beneath him,
illuminated by glowing streetlamps
and the bustle of the crowds –
sand sculptors, magicians, and street vendors
hawking their wares,
entertaining passers-by.

On hot August nights
greasy smoke clouds rise
from Thrasher's French Fry Stand
and mingle with the scent of
sweet pink cotton candy,
as the tip of his Salem Light
glows like a burning ember.

On hot August nights
the trolley bell rings out,
punctuating the thick summer air,
as the wooden boards
rattle and groan,
protesting its immense weight,
and the crowd parts to make way.

On hot August nights
he sits for hours
watching the rising high tide,
the breakers pounding the shore,
the heat lightning on the horizon,
the seagulls taking cover,
the squealing children and slurring drunks.

On hot August nights
he lights another cigarette
against the persistent wind,
closes his eyes, and is lulled to sleep…
rocking, gently rocking
to the hypnotic rhythms of the sea
at the Lankford Hotel.

## Jigsaw

I found him underground in the musty basement,
his haven from the blistering August heat.
All one thousand pieces were spread out before him
on the large mint green painted wood table.

Curious, I sat down beside him, watching
as he patiently worked, deep in concentration,
putting together interlocking cardboard cutouts,
the jutting pieces fit into matching holes.

"Start with the straight edges,
build the framework, the border.
Then observe the colors and patterns
and fill in the pieces from there," he said.

I felt the waves of teenage angst receding
as I lost myself inside that puzzle.
Calmness spread through my jumbled mind,
as I focused on the blue shades of the Amsterdam sky.

Yesterday I found that puzzle, dust on its box,
and pulled it from the musty basement shelf.
I spread the pieces out on my brown card table
and began to work the puzzle, as he once did.

The adult anxieties in my mind began to dissipate
as I searched for borders, patterns and Amsterdam skies.
Pieces perfectly aligned, my mind went blank
as I solved the jigsaw puzzle of my life.

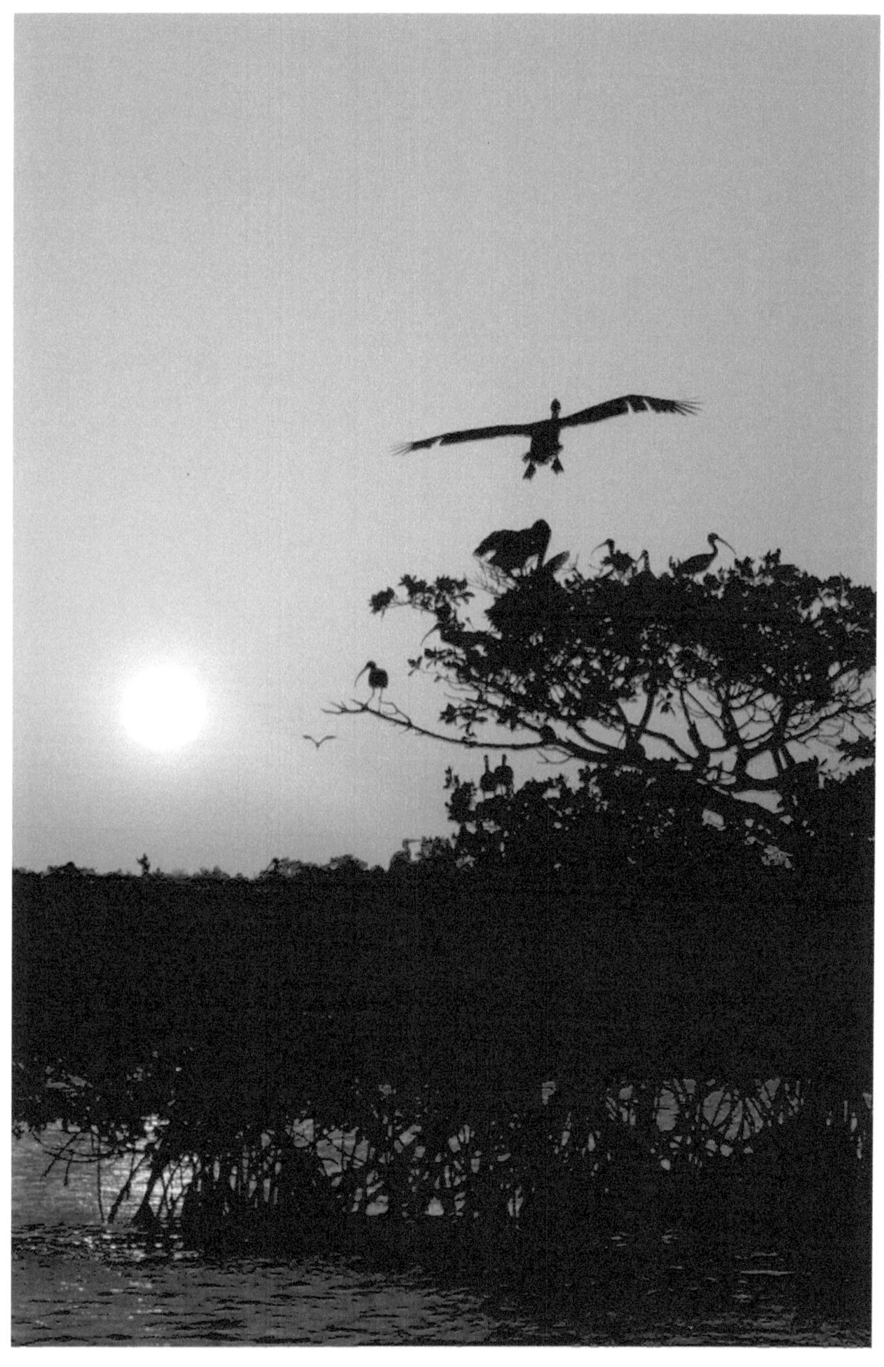

***"How blessings brighten as they take their flight."***

Edward Young

## Composers

You favored Beethoven,
passion and mystique resonating
from his thundering symphonies,
while I fancied Mozart,
with his haunting piano concertos
and complex operatic charm.
I was a quick study in classics
under your silent tutelage.

We listened to Tchaikovsky,
his proud war symphonies
with pounding drums,
thundering orchestra crescendos,
music soaring and rising,
cannonball explosions,
ascending in ultimate triumph,
fists raised in a victory celebration.

As the violins swelled on
Brahms's Hungarian Dances,
I became an elegant lady in waiting,
bedecked in hoop gowns and diamonds,
gaily twirling around the room with
my imaginary soldier hero
in a festive ballroom lit
by ten thousand candles.

Edvard Grieg brought me fantasy,
morning sunlight breaking,
innocent hatchlings chirping,
climbing treacherous mountains,
chased by unknown predators,
perhaps a grizzly bear
or an evil witch from the depths
of the mysterious Black Forest.

Ravel taught me sensuality,
though I was too young to realize
that his sensuous strains of Bolero
were weaving sultry fantasies,
building a straining crescendo,
explosive climax and resolution,
erotic and emotional,
leaving me simply craving more.

How fitting, then, that it was I
who would choose the music
for your memorial.
Sifting through your music collection,
these poignant memories swirled
and I settled on Beethoven's adagios,
the constant background music
of your life and now...

the soundtrack for your afterlife.

## **Sad Sonata**

Curved fingers on a piano
tenderly touching ivory keys.
A solemn sort of song,
a haunting melody.

This hymn is for the living,
a tribute to the dead.
I close my eyes and listen as
the passage echoes in my head.

The melancholy sonata,
devoid of lyrical words
is fading ever slowly
like a distant, calling bird.

Disconsolate chords gently nudge
a sadness deep within my soul.
My voice is mute, I cannot sing.
Thus, the story remains untold.

## The Silent Train

My mind swims with thoughts of him…
Red lights flashing, the locomotive chugs past,
transporting me back in time.

We once trudged the railroad tracks,
the crunching, coal-specked snow
beneath our cold, numb feet.
Silent, but for smoky puffs of breath
that caught and swirled upon the bitter breeze.

You showed to me that frigid February day ~
a father's love. Your smile, your simple presence
spoke more than mere words could ever say.

The shrill scream of the engine whistle
reverberates in the air.
I cannot hear it now,
but it pierces my anguished soul.

As I stand trembling by the crossing gate,
a puff of engine steam blasts my skin and rises up,
unleashed into the periwinkle summer sky.

The silent train passes…
and life pulses in my veins,
memories echo in my mind,
warm comfort envelopes my heart…

*for I know you are watching me.*

## **Ripples on the Pond**

Majestic oak limbs frame the azure sky
Dappled gold leaves alight in amber sun.
Listen to the mockingbird's mournful cry...
Foretelling, my emotions come undone.

Anguished sobs carry in the autumn breeze
Floating in the atmosphere, out of sight.
Weary victim of the cruelest disease...
Your spirit slowly faded into night.

How much longer until this pain subsides,
Until this heartbreak takes its final toll?
I walk alone, but carry you inside....
Your essence ever fused within my soul.

Grief comes in waves, like ripples on the pond...
Soothed by your gentle whisper from beyond.

## Walk into the Light

Your plight has been long, weary traveler,
But now you near your journey's end.
Though you tread through life's labyrinth,
Your future path is too hazy to portend.

The clouds of uncertainty descend
As the bell tolls solemnly at midnight.
The gates of destiny have opened wide,
Just turn and walk into the light.

Cast to the wind all of your fears;
On your nagging doubts, do not dwell.
What lies ahead may be heaven,
Or perhaps the other side of hell.

You stand on the edge of purgatory,
Its flaming inferno, a terrifying sight.
You have crossed into the other side
As you turn and walk into the light.

## **Dreams of Luminosity**

As I climb between cool pressed sheets
my worried head sinks into the pillow.
Eyes scorched from bitter tears close,
shutting out the cruelty of the day.

The opaque void of sleep descends,
spreading like black ink across my mind,
blotting out my troubles,
dissipating worries,
staving off my fears
for one more night.

The first spark of a dream ignites
within my restless brain,
a single luminous flame
sparkling like a sapphire,
beckoning me to rise up,
lighting the way for me…

And suddenly I come to life,
I am dancing…
I am singing…
I am smiling…
I am free!

Free of my anxieties,
free of tears that imprison,
free of chains that bind,
free to soar like a seagull,
free to be me!

In the sanctity of dreams
no charades, no sovereignty
govern or restrain me.
No rocks drag down my heart,
no rain falls upon my soul.
My spirit glides among the clouds,
joyous and ebullient.

When the first morning sunrays
burst from the eastern horizon,
rousing me from my slumber,
I hear a voice inside my head
reminding me I have the power
to make my dreams of luminosity
my truth and
my reality.

## Letting Go

There is nothing harder than learning to let go.
Thoughts of you cross my mind with each passing day.
I loved you more than you will ever know.

We sang endless nursery rhymes over in the meadow.
Dancing in spring gardens, we would laugh and play.
There is nothing harder than learning to let go.

Perched on your lap, we watched from our attic window
The sparkling, dazzling Fourth of July fireworks display.
I loved you more than you will ever know.

Autumn nights on the porch swing, rocking to and fro
Watching the crimson sunset over the Chesapeake Bay.
There is nothing harder than learning to let go.

You baked Christmas walnut cake as I watched it snow,
A glorious blizzard pouring from skies of gray.
I loved you more than you will ever know.

Now my tears fall to the ground as cold winds blow.
I touch your coffin one last time and kneel to pray.
There is nothing harder than learning to let go.
I loved you more than you will ever know.

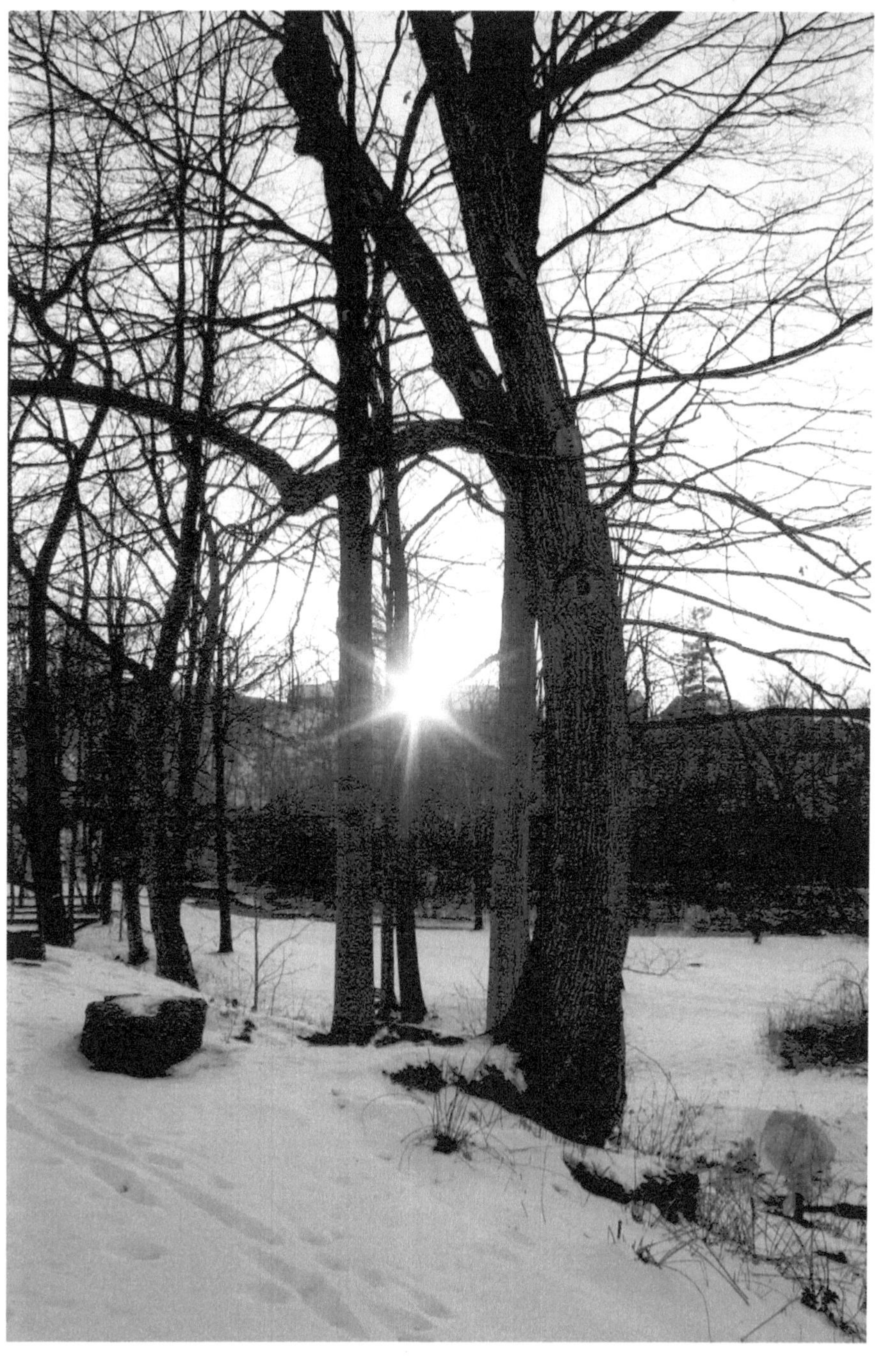

***"Look deep into nature, and then you will understand everything better."***

Albert Einstein

## Walnut Cake

Snow is falling lightly outside,
sticking to the frosty windowpanes.
The eggs, flour, and sugar have been blended,
the batter rests in the aqua ceramic bowl.

He stands in the kitchen by the sink
and wields a small knife in his weathered hands,
preparing the final ingredient with precision
as Bing Crosby croons a carol on the radio.

Chop, chop, chop...
He chops black walnuts,
tapping out a steady rhythm
on the wooden cutting board.

He folds the walnuts into the batter
and spreads it evenly with a wooden spoon.
He slides the pan into the cavernous oven,
the sounds of bells jingling in the air.

Before long, the sweet vanilla aroma
wafts through the house, with promises of
luscious walnut cake and hot black coffee ~
a Christmas morning tradition.

Chop, chop, chop…
He chopped black walnuts,
fine nut granules piled high
on the wooden cutting board.

He passed the recipe down to me,
carefully hand printed on an index card,
butter stains imprinted in the corner,
tattered and yellowed from years of use.

I try in vain to replicate his confection.
I blend the batter, chop the walnuts,
but the cake just won't come together.
It lacks one key ingredient: my father's love.

Chop, chop, chop…
I chop black walnuts.
Hot tears slide down my cheek
onto the wooden cutting board.

## **Sonnet for a Mother's Anxiety**

If I could have one wish before I die,
before I drift forever into sleep,
my children would see clearly through my eyes
my choices, bargains, promises to keep.

The labor pains of birth could not compare
to raising children in this world's unrest.
The years of worry, sadness, and despair
put my maternal instincts to the test.

I cried and prayed through anger and heartbreak.
I tried to guide you, like your harbor light.
You drifted from my reach and made mistakes.
You ruddered through rough waters, made things right.

Your smiling eyes, immortal works of art,
and gentle voices heal this mother's heart.

## **Lone Seagull's Journey**

Lost in dark clouds
of confusion
and sorrow,
one lone seagull
hurries home,
straining against the
relentless winds
of the incoming storm.

He flails his wings
with all his might,
sailing far above
the churning ocean,
across brilliant hued clouds
in a jewel-toned sky,
painted by the
dipping crimson sun.

This mighty bird,
brave of heart,
strong of wing,
pushes past the sadness
of a thousand yesterdays,
sailing into the hopes
and dreams of tomorrow,
on the promise
of a safe journey
home.

## Whitewash

Picture perfect,
it gleamed within my mind,
that Americana postcard
clapboard cottage
with white picket fences
framing lush lawns
of verdant bluegrass.

I aspired to the dream
and punched the clock,
toiling fluorescently,
racking up meal allowances
and manila accolades,
none the wiser
to your schemes…

My world was translucent,
with pasted-on smiles
and a hasty coat of
slapped-on whitewash
tempering imperfections,
the half moon of my heart
emitting a faint crimson glow.

But the bottom dropped out…
the wood warped and splintered,
its white paint peeling,
shedding layers of deceit,
the foundation cracking,
imploding concrete slabs
smashing rose colored filters.

And in the quiet of the aftermath,
tongue muted, head tilted…
my defeated eyes caught
a curlicue of hope rising
in the fading whitewash
of ash-cloaked clouds
in gray twilight skies.

## Cedar Lawn

No snow at Cedar Lawn today,
just the muggy, misty hint of rain.
No desperate sobbing or grieving from the past,
just quiet tears to soothe my heart's pain.

The green mound of your grave softly yields
under my weight as I gingerly kneel.
I touch the brass angel on your headstone
and cherish its cool metallic feel.

The weathered conch shell is still there
that I placed upon your grave a year ago ~
an iconic contrast of summer joy
amidst a blanket of pure February snow.

The sun peeks through the afternoon clouds.
I look up to the sky and manage a smile.
God's rays of hope reassure me, and I feel
your calming hand upon my shoulder all the while.

Father, I am comforted that you hear me ~
you are with me each day, wherever I may go.
Deep in my heart, you are always on my mind
through my joy and sadness, high points and low.

Now as I rise and leave your resting place today,
hear my trembling voice and the words I ask of you.
Please keep watch on me from your clouds in heaven,
with your eternal love, guide me safely through.

## **The Detour Not Taken**

My hands were trembling
as I placed my slender arm
through the loop of yours,
strong, solid, and protective.

Soft organ music swelled and echoed
through the rafters of St. Mary's
as we stood at the back of the church,
waiting for our cue.

The church bells tolled at one o'clock
as if to sound a warning.
The aisle stretched out miles before us,
as relatives and friends sat, waiting anxiously.

You looked into my brown eyes,
awash with hope and anxiety,
and whispered in my ear,
"You don't have to do this."

Your words momentarily took away my breath,
even angered me. Fighting back tears,
my cheeks flushed deep pink
and my brows furrowed in a flash.

I softly whispered your name, in protest.
I didn't know that you were trying to save me
from my fate, my destiny, that ring of fire
that I was about to walk right into.

You bent your head lower, repeated your offer.
We could just walk out that back door,
go home, pretend this all never happened.
What I didn't know is that you had a crystal ball.

I was your good, compliant daughter…
and in my only act of rebellion,
I shook my head, tilted my chin upward
and looked straight ahead.

And so we walked … the music growing louder.
I felt myself floating, surreal as if in a dream,
floating right into that ring of fire,
my destiny. *My nightmare.*

I purposely buried those fleeting seconds,
locked them away for twenty-five years.
I had erased it from my mind,
pretended that none of it ever happened.

As you lay dying in your bed years later,
I stroked your head, clumps of your hair in my hand.
You smiled weakly and reminded me
of that day that you tried to stop me, to save me.

Today the memories gnaw at me,
like a rodent chewing through a garbage bag.
And I wonder what my life would have been,
had I taken up your offer…

*had I taken that detour.*

## A Song of Peace

Hummingbird hovers, ruby-clad,
Drinking sweet nectar's fill.
Dragonfly lands on lily pad,
Summer air dank and still.
It's time to rest, evening undressed,
Soleil descends in skies of west.
It's time to rest…
It's time to rest…
Moonlight shines at nature's bequest.

Calm water ripples with worry,
Like pebbles in a pond.
Peace, infiltrate my soul -- hurry
And stir a magic wand
To calm the mind, breathe and unwind.
Let troubles fade, leave stress behind.
To calm the mind…
To calm the mind…
Troubles drift away undefined.

Serenity ebbs in my heart,
Joy flows within my veins.
Above, gray nimbus breaks apart,
Unleashing cooling rains.
The raindrops fall, melodic call,
Eroding hatred's crumbling wall.
The raindrops fall…
The raindrops fall…
Harmonic song of peace for all.

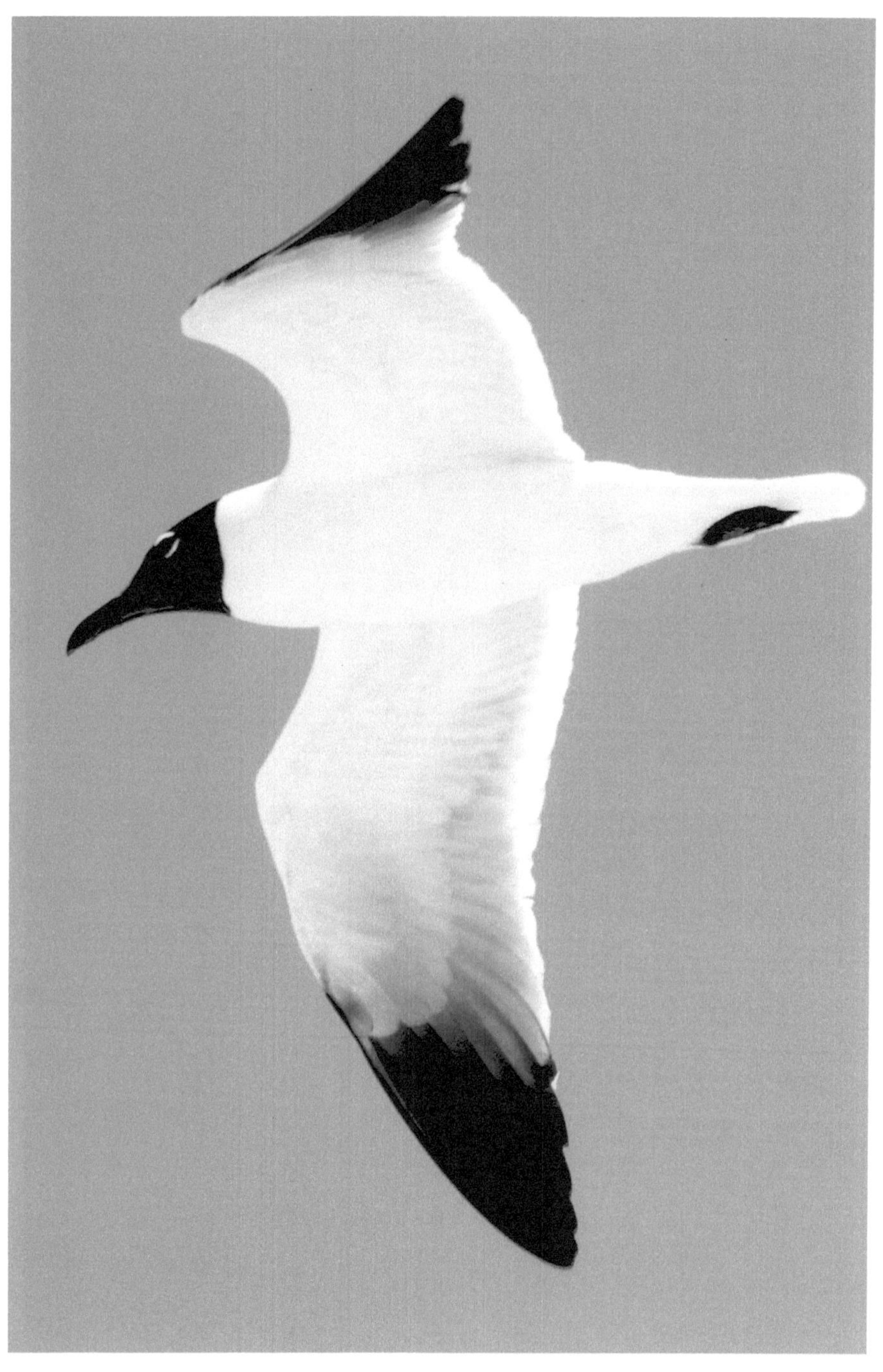

***"Death and love are the two wings that bear the good man to heaven."***

Michelangelo

## The Ukulele

Rummaging blindly through the
dusty basement bookcase,
searching hands stumble upon an odd shape.
I grasp the smooth, cool vinyl
and pull the treasure
from the murky depths.

My heart flutters at the sight
of the instrument's case.
Unzipped, immediate recognition
sparks the reels of memories
to play in my mind
like crude Technicolor film.

Muggy summer evenings,
with windows thrown wide open,
we sat on the avocado green tweed sofa
entranced by the sight of you,
strumming the nylon strings
of your tiny amber ukulele.

The chords so high, so sweet, so foreign,
seemed to swirl around the living room,
past the golden sheer curtains,
like bursts of warm sunshine
blowing in the night breeze
and floating away, up into the dark sky.

Such a dichotomy – this mighty silent man,
cradling the tiny ukulele in his large hands.
Smiling, he crooned to his children,
utterly charmed by this Hawaiian instrument
redeemed at the hardware store
with books of S&H Green stamps.

Allured by the promise of its pleasing melody,
we tiptoed through the tulips
and sat under the apple tree
by the light of the silvery moon.
We danced on beaches and sipped stardust cocktails,
serenaded by the lulling strum of your fingers.

Now silent for over forty years,
your ukulele still speaks to me.
I turn the rigid keys on the instrument's neck
to tighten its relaxed strings,
then hold it mutely in my hands.
I can still hear its harmonious songs from long ago.

Someday I will play your ukulele.
I will learn its magical secrets,
and hold this precious memory of you
close inside my aching heart…

*as I drift away to meet you*
*on Hawaiian breezes.*

## The Hills of Virginia

Slopes of malachite slalom,
stretching out endlessly,
careening past rows of stately firs,
and elderly maples, stout and strong.

The hills are dotted with birch trees,
dressed in craggy white bark coats,
notched with black lines,
as if to mark the passage of time.

Vermillion leaves once adorned the trees.
Now they are golden peanut brittle,
blown to the ground below
by cold northeasterly winds.

The skies are overcast with grey stratus,
stretching across the vast horizon,
kissing the peaks of the Shenandoah
with their sweet, wet mist.

Chipmunks scurry with acorns
as bluebirds glide across amber meadows.
Scrub jays hawk their warning,
and the fawn disappears deep into the woods.

The clouds part, and the orange sun glows,
preparing to descend into the westernmost crest,
casting its final colors across the palette of the sky
as night falls in the hills of Virginia.

## Stone Walls

Drops of poison ink
spill out my strife,
onto a tattered page
in the book of my life.

Watermarks ripple,
drowning in tears,
distorting my words,
concealing my fears.

Old limestone fence,
walls of apprehension
I have carefully built,
muddling my intentions.

I sequester myself,
stone upon stone
beneath steely gray clouds
as I sit here alone.

As the sky breaks open,
a torrent of summer rain
seeps into my pores,
soothing the pain.

Translucent dewdrops glint
when the sun pushes through,
revealing a scattering of
tiny diamonds, shiny and new.

Creeping ivory shines
a green luminescent glow,
and I see hope eternal
in a beckoning rainbow…

## **Fighting Conch**

Dawn hides in its
heavy black clouds
as the tide rolls in,
kissing the shore.
I walk alone,
pensive, pondering,
praying for you.

Please God,
let him be okay,
I fervently pled.
Just show me a sign,
I whispered
to the indifferent
sea breeze.

My eyes scanned
the steel gray horizon
and the churning tides.
A glint of gold
tumbling in the breakers
flashed in my eyes,
beckoning me.

Against whipping winds,
I bent towards
the foamy surf,
thrust my hand into
the briny, swirling water
and scooped up
my treasure.

I clasped it tight
in my dampened palm --
a fighting conch
a perfect shell,
a symbol of hope,
of perseverance,
of things to come.

You battled fiercely,
like a fighting conch....
But I never got the chance
to take you to that beach.
We never walked
in that surf together,
hand in hand.

I placed that fighting conch
on your tombstone.
It is still there
eight years later...
bleached alabaster,
tempered by ice
and unforgiving snow.

God gave me
my sign that day,
but I did not realize it
at the time....
that you would be okay,
that you would be exactly
where you should be.

You,
a perfect fighting conch,
finally at peace...
in God's kingdom.

## Only Seasons Change

The sun breaks over the mountain ridge,
Its warming rays paint the morning sky.
Clouds of cotton dot the fields of azure,
Pierced by the blue jay's wanton cry.

As I sit in your garden on the old stone bench,
Wind chimes tinkle as the March winds blow.
I wait for the blooms of daffodils to unfold,
Beautiful pastel blossoms all in a row.

But spring gives way to summer storms,
I stand here all alone in the pouring rain.
A mirage of memories burst into a rainbow,
Fragments of the past scattered in my brain.

Autumn ushers in a parade of colors, red and gold.
Pulled by gentle rhythms, the harvest moon shines bright.
It casts a silvery luminescent glow into your garden,
A perfect silhouette against your fading light.

Bare maple branches scratch against my windowpane
As frigid winter wakes me from my restless sleep.
My heart is frozen like an icicle before the thaw.
Like the heavy frosted clouds, I begin to weep.

Another year passes, my heart still bleeds for you.
It's sad to say, your fate was so rearranged.
Though seasons come and seasons go,
One thing is certain - my love for you will never change.

## The Empty Chair

Empty velvet chair
by the barren brick fireplace
beckons me to sit.

Aqua Velva scent,
cigar box stuffed with beloved
black and white photos.

Mozart sonata,
tick-tock of the mantel clock
fills the drafty air.

Curled up in the chair
I feel safe and protected,
embraced in strong arms.

I recall your face,
thin lips twist into a smile,
your laugh in my ears.

A year has passed since
you were granted angel wings.
I mourn for you still.

In the winter chill,
thoughts of you warm my numb heart…
Your chair comforts me.

## Little Turtle

A tiny head pokes out of muddy lake waters.
I can see you, I know that it is you.
Come to me, my baby turtle.
My heart swells as you swim to shore.

Stretching out your slender neck to see,
you seem to smile at me.
You take the bread right from my hand,
so gentle, so grateful for nourishment.

Delicate front paws, webbed fingers
spread and stroke the marshy grasses.
On your shell lies a carpet of fuzzy green moss
from lounging in lazy summer waters.

You let me stroke the bumps of your brown armor
and touch your pointed nose with my finger.
I talk to you soothingly as you take more bread
and look into your sea-green eyes for comfort.

Little turtle, creature sent from God,
you are a blessing in my time of sorrow.
A silent, gentle soul, you are
just like my father.

Now sated on my wheat bread,
you turn and swim away gracefully,
gliding into the black void of the lake.
I thank God for you, the simple gift of you.

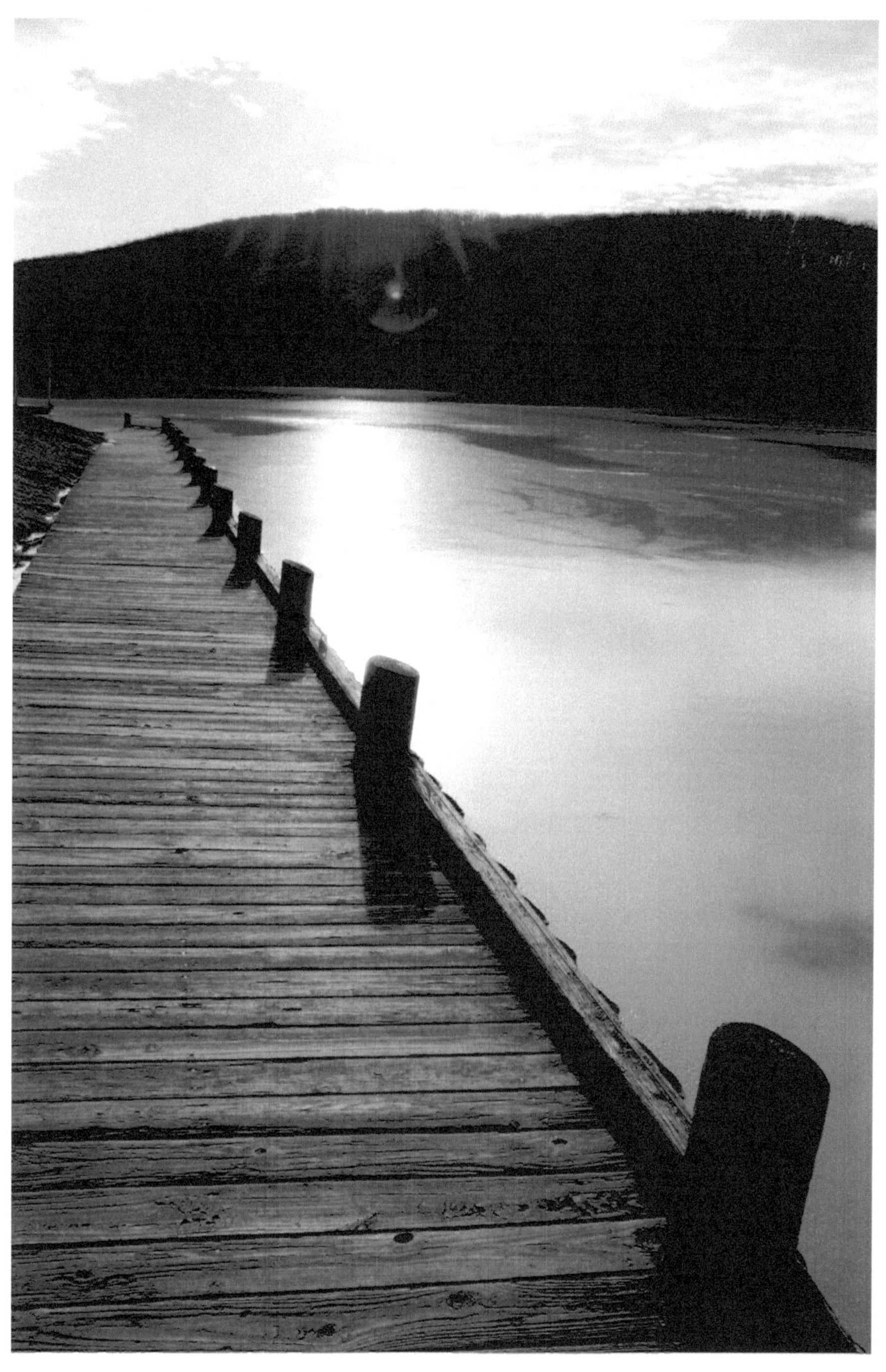

***"Live as if you were to die tomorrow. Learn as if you were to live forever."***

Mahatma Gandhi

## Hockey Lessons

Annie Green Springs warm and tipsy,
I parked my yellow Opel by the curb and
stumbled in the front door of our white duplex
that frosty night in November.

You were sitting silent in your camel recliner
watching hockey on the small color television.
The ever-present Salem dangled from your hand,
curlicue smoke slowly rising, touching the ceiling.

Instead of rushing up the narrow stairs to bed,
perhaps to avoid Mom's inevitable inquisition,
I tentatively shuffled by you unnoticed, and
lightly perched on the green and gold plaid sofa.

You didn't seem bothered by my presence.
You didn't even mind my stupid, drunken questions.
You patiently explained the rules of hockey –
icing, slashing, tripping, offsides, boarding.

You chuckled when a fight erupted, as gloves were dropped.
You expounded on the concept of the penalty box.
My intoxicated eyes struggled, but could not follow
that little black puck on the white expanse of ice.

That was the evening I fell in love with hockey,
the bright white of the rink flashing upon me,
the crisp, fast sounds of razor blades cutting the ice,
the solid crash of thick male bodies upon the boards.

I could nearly feel the chill of the ice upon my neck,
fairly smell the pungent sweat of hockey gear in my nostrils.
I became hypnotized by this winter game,
and fell asleep at your side that night.

Many years later, my life took its twists and turns.
When I would return to visit, there you were in your recliner.
We resumed our familiar comfort of watching hockey.
No longer silent, we talked of hockey, life and dreams.

Time has marched on, thirty years have passed
since my first hockey lesson that cold November night.
Now I watch hockey on my big screen high definition TV,
alone on my sofa, wrapped snugly in my robe.

I hear that familiar scraping sound of skates upon the ice,
the thud of checking bodies crashing the boards,
the whistle of the referees, the drone of the announcers,
the solid slapshot from the blue line, the air horns blasting!

Though the sounds of hockey pervade the air in my home,
my heart still feels so empty since you have gone.
A single tear slides down the curve of my cheek,
but I smile as your precious Capitals score…

*and win in overtime.*

## The Cartographer's Last Request

Long ago he etched the seas,
scaled distant mountains
and traversed dense jungles,
this drawer of lines,
wielding astrolabe and pen
with masterful precision.

A dust-laden mahogany desk
bears witness to his labors:
tarnished sextant,
musty gilt-edged tomes,
barren inkwell...
tools of his trade,
this dying art.

He whispers with gravel voice
and sense of urgency.
I lean my ear closer
with deep reverence,
straining to hear somber words
rise from his heaving chest.

"Meet me at the point of demarcation,
stand firm on the longitude of today.
Do not fall east and wallow in yesterday
or the fruitless west of tomorrows
that may never come to pass...
for the earth belongs to the living,
not to the dead."

He lies in the waning moon
of his fading twilight,
eyes dim in lined alabaster face,
frail ink-stained hands motionless.
The north arrow points homeward,
the mariner's final destiny.

I gaze upon his lithographs,
finely etched artifacts,
fingers tracing serpentine
this International Date Line...

and my mind's eye visualizes
a swim in the Indian Ocean,
a trek in snow laden peaks,
verdant African rainforests.

He leaves his legacy
inscribed in parchment,
the fruition of adventure
and colorful imagination…
masterpieces of history
bearing compass rose
and an indelible watermark,
the fertile essence of his soul.

## **Running in the Rain**

The sky is dark, the air is chilled this morn,
But the mockingbird still calls.
The pounding in my head, the sadness in my soul
Doesn't hold me back at all.

The wind, it clears my troubled mind
And chills the fever deep within my soul.
I thought my fears would wash away for good,
But I'm just left feeling weak and old.

I was running in the rain,
I was trying to ease the pain.
My legs strain to keep up the pace
As the tears run down my face.

I saw you standing there along the road
As I traveled on my way.
I stopped and looked straight into your eyes,
They were shades of green and gray.

I tried to help you find your path
Through enlightenment and song.
But when I turned around to look once more,
You were gone.

I was running in the rain,
Trying to find you once again.
How could the pouring rain feel so right
When you were nowhere left in sight?

I can't stop this feeling in my mind…
I'm afraid, but I can't say why.
I try to smile, to laugh, to play,
But it's all an act, a foolish lie.

I wish this rain would sweep me far from here,
Wash me deep into the ground.
Without you here, my life is empty, full of woe.
You were the best thing that I ever found.

But for now, I'm just running in the rain,
Trying to calm the fears within my brain.
When the heavens open up wide and pour,
My heart will mend and love once more.

Heal me, rain, and soothe my tortured soul.
Like a sacred river, baptize me.
Seep into my pores, cleanse away my sins…
Forever set my captive spirit free!

If I could ever shake this thing,
I would erase the sights I saw.
The black clouds part, sunlight filters through,
And I realize life's not so bad at all.

I'm no longer running in the rain,
Trying to kill my fears and pain.
I see your image linger in the ray of light,
And I know I am going to be all right.

## Daylight

Pushed from Mother Earth's womb,
a new day is born.
Innocent sunlight
rises like helium,
radiant,
and wraps its scorching arms
around the world.

Blossoms burst
like fireworks, shades of
red, peach, and lavender.
Delicate morning glories
kissed by dewdrops,
nurtured by hummingbirds
flitting to and fro.

The hours stretch lazily
across the sky
like tepid twilight.
The heat cascades down
into the welcoming nest
of cool green blades of grass
and complaining crickets.

Dusk draws down its shades.
The sleepy sun casts
its final encore, a fiery show
of indigo and hot pink rays
against gathering cumulus clouds,
then tucks itself
into night.

## The Healing Balm

I sit in your old velvet chair by the fireplace
Surrounded by heartache, loss, and pain.
Sifting through the old photos in your cigar box,
I take another trip down Memory Lane.

I recall when I last saw you, the sun was shining,
The luminous soft light framing your pale face.
It was New Year's Day when we said goodbye,
Then your spirit disappeared without a trace.

My heart still bleeds after being ripped apart,
Unrelenting buckets of tears I've cried.
It's been six years now since you passed away,
But I could never forget you if I tried.

The sands of time hurriedly implore me …
I'm holding on too tight to days gone by.
Like a guardian angel, you gently guide me,
Mindful that I must learn to walk before I can fly.

You are the cool breeze that ruffles through my hair,
You are the peaceful white dove perched upon my sill.
You are the hands upon my shoulder comforting me,
You are in Beethoven's music, my heart it does fill.

The memories swirl like a tornado inside my mind,
A writer spilling ink on a storm-tossed night.
Releasing my words and purging my sorrow,
I rise up to greet the new dawn's golden light.

Memories of you are a healing balm that is ordained,
Rubbed upon my broken heart so tenderly.
I will move forward without you, though it will be hard….
But I will love you and hold you inside me for eternity.

## The Walls of Camelot

Fleeting, flickering images from early childhood
replay silently in my mind
like an old black and white movie.

It was one cold November day;
I must have been around three years old.
She was standing in her ivory slip dress,
ample bosom underneath the lace outline,
in the middle of the living room.
She was ironing Daddy's work trousers,
sprinkling water on the cotton fabric
from a Pepsi bottle she kept in the refrigerator.
Steam hissed and sprayed from her iron
as she firmly pressed the seams without looking,
transfixed on the caisson and funeral car procession
that flashed across the television screen.

*Tears were streaming down her face.*

One late winter Sunday we piled into the Ford Fairlane,
took a drive for hours, it seemed.
Mommy was on a mission,
searching for the Eternal Flame
and the Tomb of the Unknown Soldier.
What were they? Barb and I weren't sure.
We trudged across the green grass of the National Cemetery,
sneakers soggy from the dew, fingers numb from the cold.
Bitter wind whipped our chapped cheeks.
The snow began to fall lightly, landing on our shoulders
as Mommy knelt and prayed among the tombstones.
We just wanted to go home.

*I remember it was St. Patrick's Day.*

One day in July, the front windows were opened wide,
the breeze billowing through the sheer curtains.
It was late in the afternoon, just before supper.
Mommy gingerly placed on the hi-fi stereo
a new vinyl disc, unsheathed from the album cover –
"Camelot", the musical soundtrack.

On the sleeve were images of pink and purple royalty.
Giggling, Barb and I danced gaily to the music,
pretending to be regal queens.
Ratty old blankets draped around our necks,
serving as our royal velvet capes.
Mommy smiled and danced with us,
and sang along, "In Camelot!"

*Tears were glistening in her eyes.*

The Warren Report occupied a critical spot
on our black aluminum book shelf,
wedged between the Kennedy biography and Webster's dictionary.
The thick, rust-colored leather volume
had mostly boring words, and some interesting pictures.
Mommy's eyes were narrowed, focused
as we gazed at the black and white snapshots --
pictures of the grassy knoll, the limousine series,
especially the one of Lee Harvey Oswald
with the gun pointed to his side.
That one mesmerized us;
we were drawn to it like magnets.

For a heavy tome with many words,
it was a fascinating book.

History is often measured
in the framework of our own memory.
Do you remember when time stood still,
in frames of black and white?

*I can still see those walls of Camelot*
*crashing down, in my mother's eyes.*

## **Unspoken**

The melancholy of the night takes hold,
The echo of your whisper lingers on.
An empty room awaits, my heart stone cold.
Ten thousand days together, now you're gone.

My mind is silent, yet tranquility
Evades. The whistle of a distant train
Unleashes fear and ambiguity
As teardrops trickle down my windowpane.

A bitter half moon lies upon my tongue.
With heavy eyes and heart I leave behind
My sentiments unspoken, songs unsung…
Forever lost, inscribed upon my mind.

This parchment paper, untouched by my pen,
No words imparted 'til we meet again.

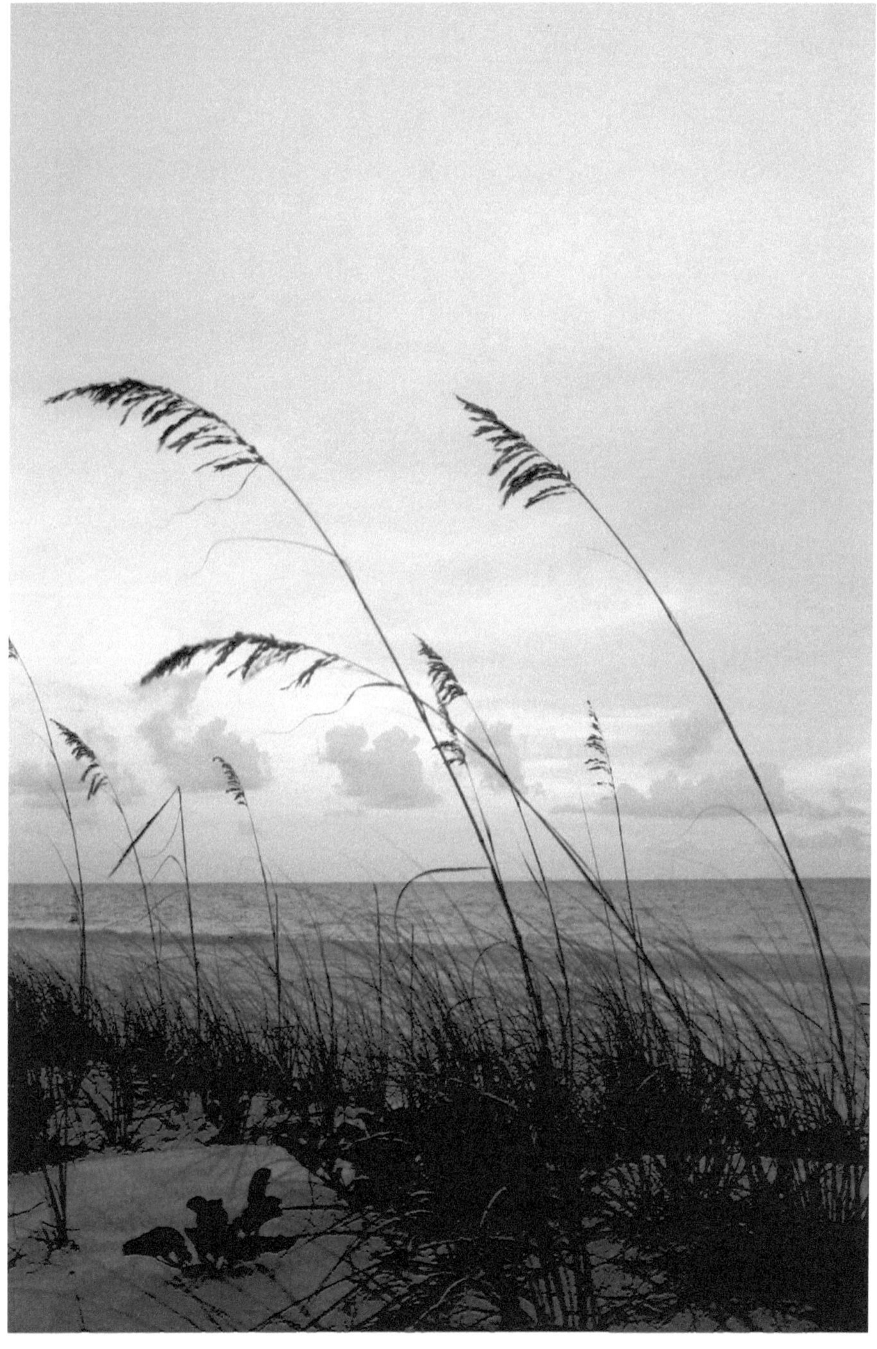

***"Don't judge each day by the harvest you reap but by the seeds that you plant."***

Robert Louis Stevenson

## **Nothing Is Perfect**

Nothing is perfect, every rose has its thorn.
The new horizon is too dark to clearly see…
But with every sunrise, a new day is born.

Watch closely, take heed as nature tries to warn.
The scorpion's sting, the poison of the honey bee…
Nothing is perfect, every rose has its thorn.

Squandered chances, my life broken and forlorn.
I hang my head in shame, crying out in misery…
But with every sunrise, a new day is born.

Suppressed tragic memories taunt and scorn,
Gremlins and ghosts of my past are haunting me…
Nothing is perfect, every rose has its thorn.

Put aside the past, for too long I did mourn,
Walking on eggshells, immersed in ambiguity….
But with every sunrise, a new day is born.

I bear the scars of one whose heart was torn,
A strong woman of grace and humility…
Nothing is perfect, every rose has its thorn.
But with every sunrise, a new day is born.

## Sidewalk Masterpieces

Festive stick people
line the summer pavement,
multi-colored rainbow arcs,
fluffy pastel clouds
and smiling yellow sun.

Joyful proclamations
etched imperfectly
by the hands of a five year old
grasping fat columns of chalk.
"I Love Daddy."

Sidewalk masterpieces
rapidly fading,
eroded by afternoon thunderstorms
and smudged by tire marks,
unlike cherished childhood memories.

## Christmas Without Pat

It's not the same at Christmas
without you, Pat.
No trinkets for the kids
when we meet at the airport.
No stockings hang on the staircase
with thick red, wooly yarn.

The refrigerator isn't stocked
chock full of Vernors soda,
cheese spread, vanilla ice cream
and your homemade salad of
macaroni, tuna, and hard-boiled eggs
that none of us can replicate.

The smiling white snow bears no longer
keep guard atop the china cabinets.
The creepy green Christmas troll
with the hammer has long been discarded.
Your gay carolers with ringlets
and red velvet have gone missing.

The Christmas tree stands tall,
but no stacks of presents surround it.
The air is silent and heavy,
no Christmas music wafting through the air.
The scent of roast beef and homemade spaetzle
have dissipated long ago.

Your black winter boots no longer
stand in the garage, waiting for snow duty.
Your colorful fur jackets are gone
from the hallway closets.
We don't even bother to light the fireplace
in the evenings, not even candles.

The clink of ice cubes in your glass of J&B scotch
no longer echoes through the living room in the evenings.

No curlicue of smoke rises from
the ever-present Kent in your absent hand.
Only the faint stench of those cigarettes
still permeates every fabric in the house.

You don't ask us the trivia questions
from your daily calendar each morning
or scramble to complete the Jumble puzzle
at the crack of dawn.
Domino tiles no longer smack upon
the wooden kitchen table at six a.m.

Christmas has come and gone twice without you.
The gray Michigan skies are getting bleaker,
the holidays less special.
As I walk the street, in the bitter cold
of New Year's Eve, I pass your neighbor's house,
Christmas lights reflecting in the glistening snow.

The tears sting the corner of my eyes
as I wonder where you are, how you are.
Life on the outside goes on,
we've turned the page on another year...
but it's not the same at Christmas
without you, Pat.

## Deserted Beach

I stand here
alone on this deserted beach,
watching the sun rise
in a glorious burst
of orange and pink,
heralding the new day.

I greet the morning
with a broken spirit.
My heart is bleeding, empty,
battered by the storms of life,
dragged across the coral reef
and left for dead
on this barren shore.

But the waves continue
to crash down…
the surf breaking,
casting broken shells
against my ankles,
drowning out my
futile wails of anguish.

I've lost my father,
my rock, my soul…
my anchor in this world
of unrest and strife.
The wounds are so raw,
the hurt so fresh,
the grief nearly unbearable.

Sorrow and loss
rain down
from my tired eyes,
my salty tears
mingling with the briny sea.

A gust of wind ruffles my hair,
a gentle whisper.
I feel my father's spirit
standing beside me
in my unrelenting pain …
touching my shoulder,
guiding me,
comforting me.

The warmth of the sun
kisses my cheeks,
fills my soul,
lifting me up
and reminding me
that though I may feel lonely…

*I am never alone.*

## Turbulence

I am sleeping lightly
in a tranquilizer-like haze
far above the bands of clouds
traveling 500 miles per hour
without a care.

I hear the chime above my earphones
as seat belt light flashes on
the pilot's voice drones overhead
about a line of thunderstorms
over the South Carolina mountains.

The turbulence hits hard
bumping, tripping, bending us
like a cruel rollercoaster ride
without a track or course
as I cover my glass of water with my hand.

Other passengers tense and panic
gripped with fear and anxiety
concerned hands clutching armrests
but I am calm and at peace
ready to go down if it is to be.

I imagine the coming pandemonium
as I listen to meditative music
the plane slipping into the frigid ocean
as water fills my lungs
I will go to meet my maker.

I can see white light behind closed eyelids
I feel my father's big warm arms around me
and I am not afraid in these fleeting moments
as I finger my golden Crucifix…

*No, I am not afraid to die.*

Then I glance over at my daughter
beside me, fear awash in her big brown eyes
I reach over and grip her small cold hands
until the turbulence subsides,
we exhale, not afraid
not ready to die…

*Not just yet.*

## Oxford Summer

The day you left Miami for your summer in Oxford
I clung to you at the gate and said goodbye as
pangs of guilt clawed me and tears stung me.
By the time your plane departed, crossing the Atlantic,
I lay on my sofa, inconsolable
as the rain wept and the thunder crashed outside.

Eager at first, you then felt reluctant –
perhaps scared to spread your fledgling wings.
The house was empty without your loud, thumping music.
My heart was aching for your smile.
I played your favorite Linkin Park songs endlessly,
crying as I scrubbed the tile floors.

The day we took the Virgin train from London into Oxford,
my stomach churned, my heart nearly thumped out of my chest.
We walked the venerable campus of St. Michael's, searching for you.
The sight of you, glorious you, took my breath away.
Basking in the warmth of your newfound happiness,
you hugged your new friends goodbye. I realized you blossomed.

Rich, poignant memories of your Oxford summer
etched in your mind, in your heart.
Cherish them forever, my dear.
Never let them go.

## Dusk Has Fallen

Dusk has fallen, here comes the night.
Raspberry skies, summer delight,
Full moon shines overhead so bright,
Fireflies blinking their Morse code light.

Shooting stars streak with fiery flare.
Dusk has fallen, here comes the night.
Cricket lullabies fill the air.
Scent of lavender in my hair.

Flash of the lighthouse beckons me,
Glowing sentinel of the sea.
Dusk has fallen, here comes the night
Shrouded in hope and mystery.

Torch lamps flicker and luminesce.
Warm winds on skin, a sweet caress,
Sun sinks down as the clouds digress.
Dusk has fallen, here comes the night.

## **Blind Faith**

Steely gray storm clouds
consume my days,
unleashing torrents of rain
and howling winds
as I search endlessly
for you.

My tunnel vision
escalates the terror
stirring in my chest --
rising, cresting,
like the raging tide.

Blind faith pushes me forward,
down that darkened stone path,
crossing through foreboding forests,
pushing against fierce winds,
still searching for you.

Up ahead, a light beckons --
distant, now growing nearer --
as I tread this broken trail
in the autumn of my life,
focusing on the black silhouette,
praying that the figure before me
is you.

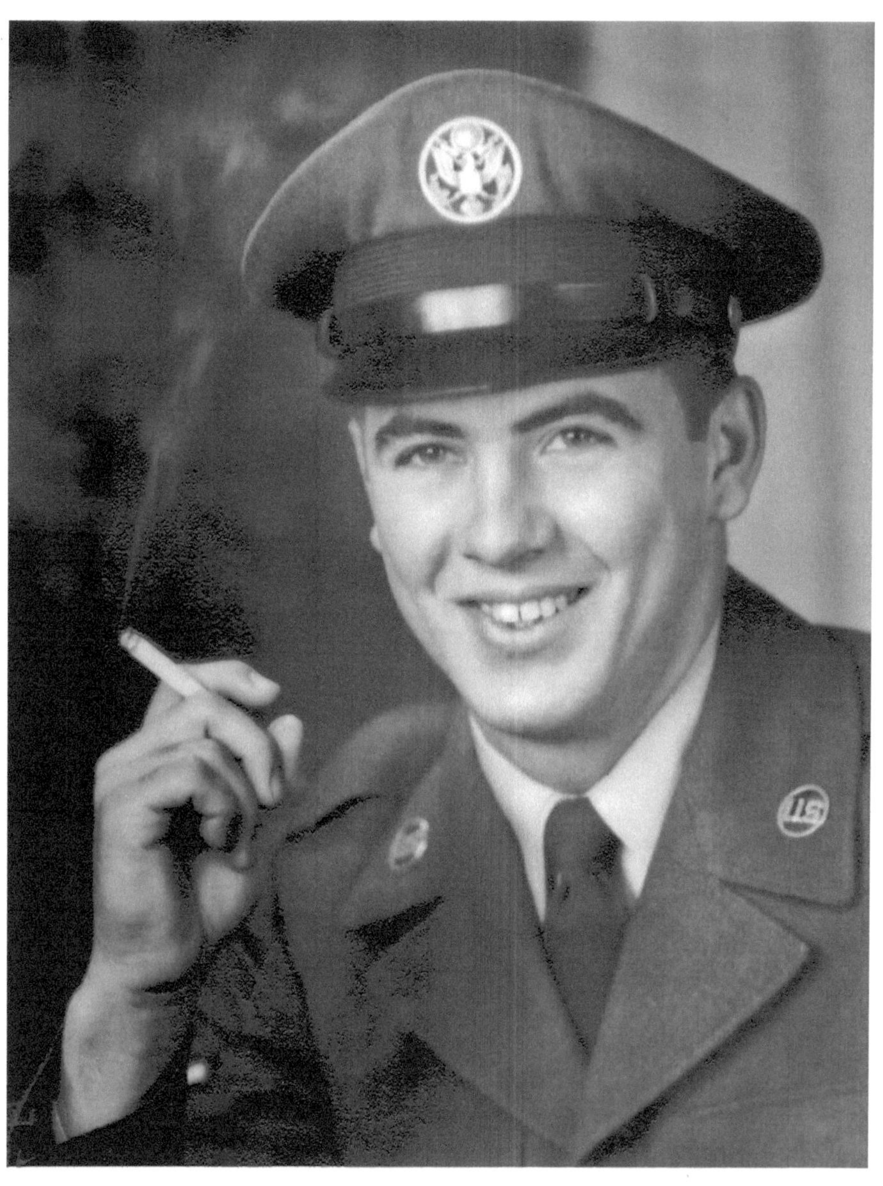

***"The dawn is not distant, nor is the night starless; love is eternal."***

Henry Wadsworth Longfellow

## Pearls from My Father

It is hard to believe that it has been over eight years since my father left this world for the green pastures of heaven. I miss my father every day of my life, but I always seem to miss him most during the Christmas holidays. All it takes is a song, a movie, the sound of bare tree limbs scratching the windowpane, the sight of a brilliant red cardinal... and Dad is with me, beside me, consoling me. Simple holiday tasks such as testing the Christmas tree lights and chopping the walnuts finely for my cheese ball cause my joyous mood to instantly turn to melancholy. Suddenly, that hidden pain comes bubbling up from an emotional wellspring deep within my soul, and the tears for my father fall upon my cheeks.

I can still vividly picture a multitude of memories we made together at the holidays, not only with our family of seven, but also with the extended Keller family. Dad was one of fourteen children who grew up during the Great Depression. As a result, I was blessed to have a multitude of aunts, uncles, cousins, and second cousins in my life. It was a grand tradition on Christmas night for everyone to gather at our matriarch Nanny's tiny second floor apartment on Baltimore Street. The brothers and sisters would join hands, dance around the apartment singing old songs after imbibing in holiday punch. Imagine how loud that must have been for the poor neighbors downstairs! But there was one Christmas that my father was singing and dancing a bit more animated than usual. I remember my mother took the keys to the Ford Fairlane and drove home very tight-lipped, gripping the wheel as a light snow fell. This was very unusual, as my father always drove, especially in the snow.

The next day we asked what was wrong with Daddy, as he spent all day in bed. My mother tersely said he had the "Hong Kong Flu." I figured out many years later that this was code for "hangover." No cure, maybe a little hair of the dog? I now know that calling a doctor would have been pointless... he would have said "just take two aspirin and call me in the morning."

My Dad was a fairly quiet and patient man. I have no doubt that there were many Christmas eves that he probably spent half the night in the cold basement assembling just about every type of toy from dollhouses to bicycles. I am certain that he must have encountered situations in which the directions were not included. I can just imagine him grumbling, "This is ridiculous!" But he did it all for his family, and he never managed to disappoint in the Santa department.

There was one year in particular when I was very young that Christmas was rapidly approaching, and my father had not bought a Christmas tree. The details are a bit fuzzy, but I can certainly remember being very upset that there was no beautiful tree to gaze upon with great hope and happiness. And... if we had no Christmas tree, where was Santa to put all the gifts? Obviously, this must have been during some tough financial times we were going through. Then one evening a few days before Christmas, there was a knock on the door. Outside stood several aunts and uncles, bursting into Christmas carols as the snow swirled around them on the front porch. They proceeded to drag a huge pine tree into our house. In a matter of hours, they had decked out that scraggly pine tree with lights, ornaments and a white star on top. I suspect that a few whiskey sours may have been involved, but I vividly remember squealing with joy at the scene! Family always took care of family.

These poignant memories are just a few of many that are seared forever in my mind. Such a dichotomy, that they bring both joy and pain simultaneously. I have learned to let those emotions flow, to get beyond the heartache and to listen to the message my father is sending to me from far beyond. I truly believe that he is telling me to cherish yesterday, dream tomorrow, but to live today. These pearls of wisdom sustain me, like manna from heaven. May this be my mantra for each day.

Peace and happiness to my family and my friends, on this day and always!

## ~ EPILOGUE ~

"Cherish yesterday, dream tomorrow, live today."

~ Richard Bach, "Jonathan Livingston Seagull."

This quote is especially meaningful for me, because my father loved the soundtrack from the movie, and shared this with me as a child. The words and the music are still a great source of inspiration for me, to this day.

*Daddy,*
*you are on my mind every single day,*
*you will live forever in my heart.*

*Thank you for being*
*my guardian angel*
*through both happy*
*and difficult times.*
*I placed my trust in you,*
*and you showed me the way.*

*So until we meet again,*
*know how much I love you!*

Colleen M. Breuning © 2011

## About the Author

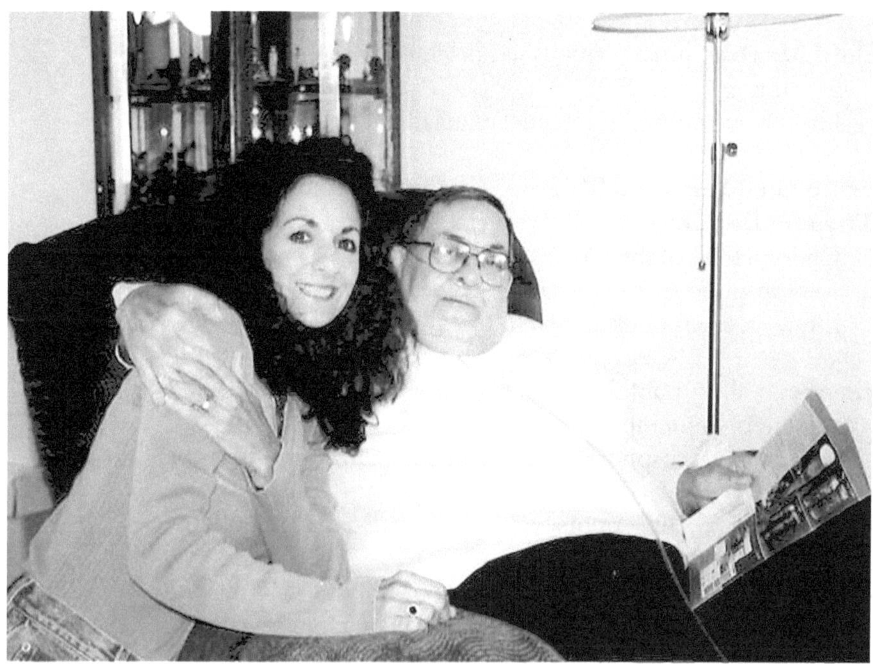

Colleen Marie Keller Breuning was born and raised in Hagerstown, Maryland. She has lived in various parts of the country, including Oklahoma and Florida, and she has recently relocated to Northern Virginia. She received her BBA in Human Resource Management from Florida Atlantic University in 1990, and has had a career in the accounting and medical fields.

Though she began writing poetry as a child, Colleen returned to writing after her father's death in 2003. She has been published in various print and online publications, and she is the owner and editor of Blue Turtle Crossing E-Zine.

Photography is one of Colleen's great passions, and her work has been featured in various publications and websites. Her intense love of nature flows forth in her breath-taking images of sunsets, animals and landscapes. She never travels anywhere without one of her Nikon cameras in hand.

In addition to writing poetry and photography, Colleen enjoys music, travel, cooking, red wine, laughter, chocolate, and cats (but not necessarily in that order). She is happily married to her soulmate Dan, and she is blessed with two children and two mischievous cats Tommy and Jordan, who are a constant source of entertainment.

## Credits, Footnotes and Links

**Cold Marble**, p. 13 ~ published in Phosphorescence Magazine, 2nd edition, June 2007
http://www.phosphorescencemagazine.com/

**From the Maryland Skies**, p. 17; **Only Seasons Change**, p. 53; **The Healing Balm**, p. 80 ~ special credit and thanks to Cheryl Holtz of the Creative Poetry Corral. These poems were inspired by collaborative lines from this poetry site.
http://www.friendburst.com/CreativePoetryCorral/

**Jigsaw**, p. 33 ~ published in Phosphorescence Magazine, 3rd edition, September 2007.
http://www.phosphorescencemagazine.com/

**Sad Sonata**, p. 39 ~ published in Ya'Sou E-zine, Fall 2006.

**Sonnet for A Mother's Anxiety**, p. 51 ~ published in Ya'Sou E-zine, June 2006; Phosphorescence Magazine, 3rd edition, September 2007.
http://www.phosphorescencemagazine.com/

**Whitewash**, p. 53 ~ published in Alabaster & Mercury E-zine, February 2011.
http://www.alabasterandmercury.com/

**The Empty Chair**, p. 68 ~ published in Ya'Sou E-zine, June 2007; Pink Mouse Pub, April 2006.
http://pinkmouseonline.com/

**Little Turtle**, p. 69 ~ published in Pink Mouse Pub, April 2007.
http://pinkmouseonline.com/

All photographs in this publication, including the cover photograph, were taken by Colleen Keller Breuning © 2011, All Rights Reserved. However, there is one notable exception: "**Dress Blues**." This photograph was inherited from the Keller family archives, and it has been released for re-print courtesy of Gloria L. Keller.

www.ingramcontent.com/pod-product-compliance
Lightning Source LLC
LaVergne TN
LVHW091012080826
845145LV00003B/1238

* 9 7 8 0 9 8 3 6 0 7 2 0 5 *